Tinashe Williamson

Handbook for Young Anti-Racists

Illustrated by
Thea Jacobsen

Translated from the Norwegian by Matt Bagguley

ig KIDS

New York, NY

For India and Ziggy

IgKids is an imprint of Ig Publishing, Inc.
Box 2547
New York, NY 10163
www.igpub.com

ISBN: 978-1-632461-64-3

"In a racist society, it is not enough to be non-racist. We must be anti-racist."

ANGELA DAVIS

I DIDN'T MEAN ANY HARM
WHERE ARE YOU REALLY FROM?
I WAS ONLY JOKING!
WHY DO WE ALWAYS HAVE TO TALK ABOUT RACE?
DON'T BE SO OFFENDED

TINASHE. 39 years old. Norwegian with Zimbabwean ancestry. Lives with her husband, and their two daughters in Norway.

"I like being with my friends, cooking and listening to music!"

As a child, I always found racism difficult to talk about. Whenever I told someone that I had experienced racism, I felt like I was reminding them that I was different. I was terrified that they would look at me in the same way as the people I was talking about; that they would also see me as inferior because of the color of my skin.

I noticed that the adults around me found racism difficult to talk about, too, and I felt shame whenever I mentioned it around them.

So, for many years, I stayed quiet, biting my tongue every time I heard a racist comment. I accepted people saying things like, "I didn't mean any harm," "can't you take a joke?" and "don't get so offended." But not saying anything made me feel small and insigificant.

If you think of a racist comment as a raindrop, one won't make you wet. But 10,000 raindrops will leave you soaked. There are many people in this world who have been very wet for a very long time!

With this book, I want to make it a easier for kids like you to talk about and understand racism. I want to show you how we can all make a difference by fighting racism together, and become active anti-racists! Dialogue is the way people become closer, and make the world a better place.

I find writing a book quite scary. But I am doing it anyway, both for my children, and for you, the children of the world.

And because you children are our future, I have brought some kids with me who are the same age as you, to help show you what it means to be an anti-racist. Let's meet them now!

5

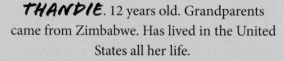 **THANDIE.** 12 years old. Grandparents came from Zimbabwe. Has lived in the United States all her life.

"I love dancing and playing basketball. At school, my favorite subjects are English and science. I hate math!
I live with my mom, dad and little sister."

ANTON. 12 years old. Mother's family is from Ukraine, father's family is from Poland. Has lived in the United States all his life.

"If it was up to me, I would play baseball every single day! My favorite subject at school is gym, and my favorite food is pizza. I live with my dad, stepmom and my two brothers."

VAISHALI. 13 years old. Both sides of her family came from India. Has lived in the United States all her life.

"I play the violin on Tuesdays, and soccer on Wednesdays and Saturdays. I like all my subjects at school, especially social studies and math. I live with my mom, dad and big brother, who can be so annoying sometimes!"

LINDA. 12 years old. Parents came from Germany. Moved to the United States with her mother, father and sister when she was five years old.

"I do freestyle dancing and love, love, tacos! At school I like music and history. But what I like best is just hanging out with my friends."

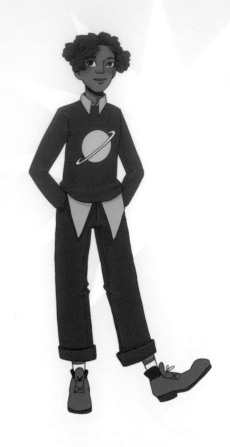

JASMINE. 13 years old. Parents are from Vietnam. Moved to the United States with her mother and father when she was three.

"I love playing the piano and riding my bike. I go riding every day when the weather is good. Falling off my bike is how I broke my arm! My favorite food is pizza without meat, because I'm a vegetarian."

SAMMY. 12 years old. Both of his parents were born in the US. Sammy is bi-racial. His father is Black and his mother is white. Sammy has lived in the United States all his life.

"I love skiing and playing the guitar. My dream is to become an astronaut and to one day walk on Mars. I love math, but hate social studies because I find history so boring. I live with my mom, dad and two sisters."

ZACK. 13 years old. Adopted from Colombia. Came to the United States as a one-year-old.

"I play tennis and love running. At school I really like English and chemistry. I'm also really interested in fashion, and want to be a hairdresser when I grow up. I live with my mom and sister, who is also adopted."

FATIMA. 12 years. Parents are from Yemen. Has lived in the United States all her life.

"I think school is fun and I want to be a doctor or scientist when I grow up! I live with my mom, dad and five siblings, two brothers and three sisters. We can get very loud in a restaurant!"

"I have a dream that my four children will one day live in a nation where they will not be judged by the color of their skin, but by the content of their character."

DR. MARTIN LUTHER KING JR.

RACISM AND ANTI-RACISM — WHAT EXACTLY ARE THEY?

RACISM is when a person or group is treated worse than another person or group because they have a different skin color, dress differently or possess different physical characteristics.

Some people believe that who a person is can be determined simply by the color of their skin. "This cannot be true," you say, but sadly it is. These people have a *preconceived* idea of how people with a certain skin color behave, how they think and what they think and judge everyone with that skin color the same way.

Becasue of these *racist* beliefs, they will "pre-judge" that person before they have said or done anything; before they have talked about what they like doing in their free time, or share what they think about the climate crisis; before they have shared their opinion about a TikTok video, or told them which football team they root for.

As a society, we cannot accept this kind of thinking! But what can we do about it? What can you and I do to make the world a kinder and more tolerant place to live? A place where our actions and opinions and thoughts are what matter, not the color of our skin, or where we originally came from?

WE MUST BECOME ANTI-RACISTS!

Being *anti-racist* means that you work actively against racism. In previous generations, people such as Rosa Parks and Dr. Martin Luther King, Jr. famously tried to do something about racism in society. Their goal was to ensure that all people were treated equally.

While we have come a long way since the days of Dr. King and Rosa Parks, we are not yet at the finish line. So to keep the fight against racism going so that we can create a more just world, we are passing the baton to you, our young anti-racists!

TINASHE: I have experienced a lot of racism in my life, especially when I was a kid like you. But my most difficult encounters with racism have been the conversations I've needed to have with my own children. As a mother, I've had to tell them that there are people out there in the world who will not like or accept them, and people who will think that they are inferior. Simply because of their skin color!

We cannot change anything without acknowledging the racism in our world, and today it is more important than ever to use our voices to stand up for what we believe is right. Only togther will we be able to do something about racism. We must all contribute. You are the future, and I'm sure you'll do a better job than many of us who came before.

YOU CAN DO IT!

Before We Start, A Few Facts...

The word *racism* has roots that go all the way back to 1859, when the English biologist Charles Darwin wrote the book, *On the Origin of Species*. In the book, Darwin described how plants and animals that had developed to be most suited to the environment in which they lived had the best chance of passing on their characteristics and traits to their offspring. He called this the *theory of evolution*.

While Darwin's theory only applied to plants and animals, it was eventually used to distinguish between different "human races," and to define which of them had best adapted to their enviroment. (This was not what Darwin had intended his theory to be used for.) Since many scientists of Darwin's time lived in Europe and where white, they assumed that white people were the strongest and most intelligent of the races. We call this type of belief *racist*.

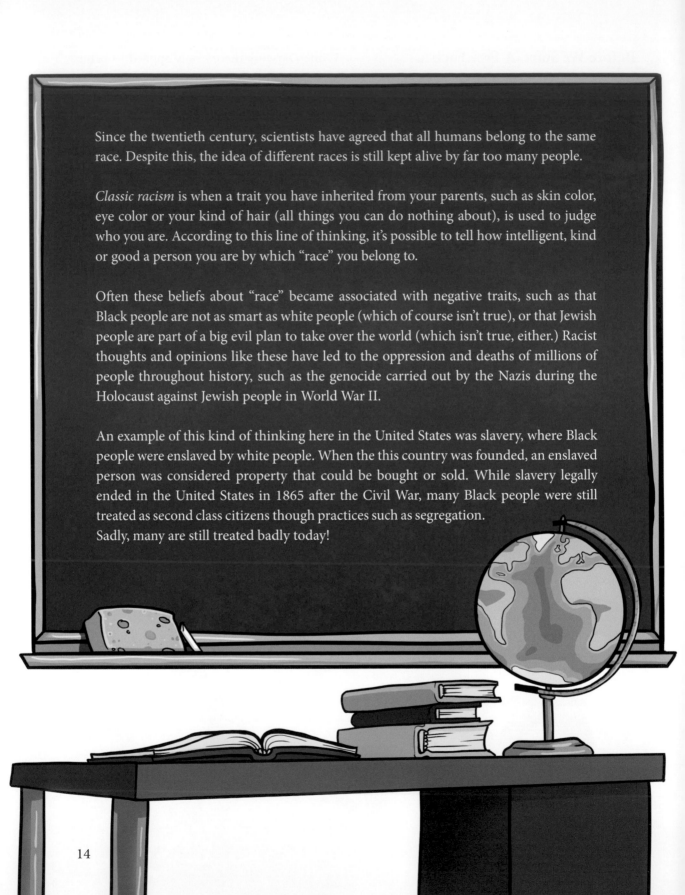

Since the twentieth century, scientists have agreed that all humans belong to the same race. Despite this, the idea of different races is still kept alive by far too many people.

Classic racism is when a trait you have inherited from your parents, such as skin color, eye color or your kind of hair (all things you can do nothing about), is used to judge who you are. According to this line of thinking, it's possible to tell how intelligent, kind or good a person you are by which "race" you belong to.

Often these beliefs about "race" became associated with negative traits, such as that Black people are not as smart as white people (which of course isn't true), or that Jewish people are part of a big evil plan to take over the world (which isn't true, either.) Racist thoughts and opinions like these have led to the oppression and deaths of millions of people throughout history, such as the genocide carried out by the Nazis during the Holocaust against Jewish people in World War II.

An example of this kind of thinking here in the United States was slavery, where Black people were enslaved by white people. When the this country was founded, an enslaved person was considered property that could be bought or sold. While slavery legally ended in the United States in 1865 after the Civil War, many Black people were still treated as second class citizens though practices such as segregation.
Sadly, many are still treated badly today!

Now, you're probably wondering what any of this has do with you. You might think that slavery was something that happened in the past, before you or your parents or your grandparents were even born. You might think that since your family never enslaved people, that the practice doesn't involve you.

In truth, the effects of slavery still exist in this country, particularly for many Black people who still suffer ecomonic, educational and health hardships due to slavery.

How did slavery come to be in the United States?

Slaves—who we now call *enslaved people* to show that they were people who were forced into slavery against their will—were kept by many civilizations in history. There were enslaved people in ancient Babylon, anicent Greece and throughout the Roman Empire. In the Middle Ages, there was a slave trade in Europe, Africa and Asia.

The most well-known slave trade took place between the 1500s and 1800s. Back then, there were no proper maps, and it was common for people, especially Europeans, to venture out in large ships to "discover" the world.

When the Europeans first came to Africa and America, they believed they had discovered totally new places, and that it was okay for them to act like these places belonged to them, despite the fact that people had already been living there for a very long time! (These original inhabitants are known as *indigeneous* people.)

These new lands which the Europeans "conquered" were called colonies. Eventually, the whole American continent was colonized—in other words conquered—by France, Portugal, Spain and Great Britain. Large parts of Africa were conquered by several other European countries, including Denmark.

This colonization became the start of the modern slave trade. Because the European colonists needed people to work on their cotton and sugar plantations, they began shipping Black African people to America. The African enslaved people were considered the property of the white plantation owners. They were forced to engage in backbreaking work, without pay, in poor conditions.

Common to all the stories about the slave trade is the fact that those who own land have the power—the power to decide who gets something and who doesn't. Back then, and even today, that power resides mainly with white people.

The slave trade in the United States continued until it was banned during Abraham Lincoln's presidency in the 1860s. Nevertheless, Black Americans are still treated like second class citizens today. As a matter of fact, some white Americans still believe that this country is for whites only.

Structural racism

What Black Americans experience nowadays is called *structural racism*. And it is not limited to the United States, but can be found throughout the world. But what does the term actually mean?

The word *structural* comes from the word structure, which refers to how something is built or constructed. A structure can be something like a jungle gym, for example. The person who built the jungle gym may have designed it to work for the majority, and built it so that it is good for everyone. However, those who are different than the majority may find it difficult or impossible to climb. So even if they try very hard, they likely won't get very far because even though it's open to all and everyone is allowed to use it, the jungle gym isn't made for them.

It's the same with larger and more complicated structures, like school or healthcare. In the United States, there are rules, laws and customs that give an unfair advantage to some groups, while discriminating against other groups, all based on race. Structural racism harms Black and brown people in many ways, including their physical and mental health, education and how much money they make!

STRUCTURAL RACISM CAN BE

- That you struggle more at school than the other students because you don't get help with your homework at home.

- That you're more likely to end up in a criminal environment because there are no good leisure activities in your local community.

- That you find it harder to get a job because you have a foreign-sounding name.

Talk among yourselves

Have you or anyone you know experienced structural racism?

THIS IS PRETTY COMPLICATED STUFF. PERHAPS AN EXAMPLE WILL MAKE THINGS EASIER

Three years ago, a boy from Mexico came to the United States as a refugee with his family. He is now 14 years old, goes to school and has learned English very quickly. But his parents still struggle to speak English, so they cannot help him with his homework and school assignments. The boy is very smart and enjoys school, but because he has three younger siblings and also has to help in his father's store, he is never able to do his homework in peace and quiet. As a result, his grades are low.

Most of the kids in his school have similar backgrounds. Their parents can't speak English, and their grades are poor. They also can't get the help they need because most of their teachers don't speak Spanish.

*Struggling at school and feeling hopeless, the boy starts participating in criminal activities with some of his friends, and is eventually caught and arrested by the police. Many of the people who hear about the boy's story think: "Typical. So many children from immigrant families do badly at school and become criminals. That's why we need to close our borders! We can't let **them** in."*

Our example shows how the *system*, in this case the school system, is constructed in a way that makes it difficult for this boy, and others like him, to succeed. The boy is smart, yet because he can't get the proper help at home and in school, his grades suffer, and he eventually starts to commit crimes because he feels like there is nothing else he can do.

Many people believe that the rules and laws are the same for everyone. While that is true, the problem is that the starting point isn't the same for everyone, especially those with a different or poor background. The jungle gym may be designed for everyone, but that doesn't mean everyone is able to climb it!

WHITE PRIVILEGE

There are often no bad intentions behind the fact that some people have an easier climb up the jungle gym than others. It is simply because the structure was designed for the majority, who are often unaware that it excludes others who are different from them.

When it comes to race, we call this *white privilege*. As a white person, you perhaps never considered that things that were easy for you might be hard for others, because you never had to think about it. It's like playing video games at different levels of difficulty. The white player might play on the lowest setting, and think it's the only setting in the game, while the player with brown or black skin has to play on the highest setting. The brown or black skinned player might still do well, and perhaps even beat the white player, but it will be much harder for them to do so.

That's why talking about structural racism and white privilege with everyone you know, no matter their skin color, is so important. By simply understanding that the system was created for a specific group of people, we can start to build structures that everyone is able to use.

Some examples of what we're talking about...

William and Asim have the same education and both received good grades in school. After they graduate, they apply for the same type of jobs. But while William receives twenty interviews, Asim only gets one, because he has a foreign-sounding name. Since Wiliam has twenty interviews, there is a much greater chance of him getting a job than Asim. This makes it easier for William to save money, buy a nice apartment and own a car. While they have the same educational background, Asim can't get do as well as William because he gets so few interviews, which means he will likely have to accept a job with a much lower salary—if he can even get a job!

While the system may be designed for everyone, William, just because of his name, benefits the most from using it. This is what's scary about white privilege and structural racism: that the differences you experience early in life, things you have no control over, can follow you into adulthood. What might seem like a trivial detail—such as your name—can have major consequences for your life, and can be passed from one generation to the next. That is why it's so important for us to understand white privilege and to fight structural racism!

FATIMA: My brother Erfan worked as an assistant in a nursing home. He was a good employee, but often had to deal with elderly people who didn't want him looking after them because he was Arab. They would often say that was "not an American." It eventually became such a problem that he was given fewer and fewer shifts. In the end, he had to quit.

ZACK: But didn't anyone say something to the people in the nursing home? And why did the nursing home stop giving Erfan shifts even though he was a good employee?

FATIMA: I don't think the staff had the understanding or desire to deal with it. It was easier for them to call Peter or Lisa, who were assistants at the same nursing home, both of whom were white.

TINASHE: Peter and Lisa didn't know that they were given more shifts than Erfan because of the color of their skin. This is an example of white privilege. By being aware of your privilege, you can become part of the solution!

If you were Peter or Lisa and were aware of your white privilege, what would you have done?

- Would you have spoken to Erfan and told him that you thought he was being treated unfairly, and ask if he would like to take some of your shifts?

- Would you have told the nursing home management that the shifts ought to be distributed equally between the assistants?

- Would you have asked for a meeting with the management to discuss what Erfan was experiencing and demand that things be done to make the workplace safe and free of racism?

19

DID YOU KNOW that "racism" comes from the word "race" which was originally used when talking about animals? Biologically, there are in fact no different human races. We are just one big race, all of us. So it's actually wrong to use that word.

Let's say someone decides that people with blonde hair suck and people with brown hair are cool. And your mom and dad both have blonde hair, and you happen to have been born like that, too, which means you are treated as inferior to those with brown hair. It all makes no sense of course! Since we know that we're all the same on the inside, why is it that some people are treated worse than others, for something they can't do anything about? For something that says nothing about who they are?

Exercise

Looking back at where you came from can be exciting! Draw a family tree and see how far back you can trace yourself. Where did your ancestors come from? Maybe they lived somewhere other than the United States? Interview your parents and grandparents to find out more!

21

LINDA: I hear what you're saying, but I'm still having a hard time understanding exactly what racism is.

THANDIE: What shocks me the most is that people have known for over 100 years that we are all the same on the inside, and yet racism still exists today.

LINDA: Have you experienced racism?

THANDIE: My whole family has experienced it, as have all my Black and Brown friends. I could give you so many examples, but one I remember is from when I was a kid and we were on a bus and a white lady told my mom that we should all go back

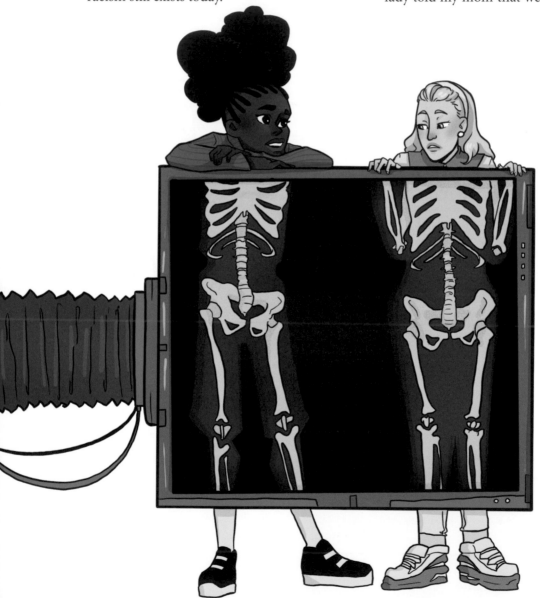

to where we came from, even though I was born and raised in the United States, as were my parents. My mom told this lady that this wasn't a nice way to talk to people, but the lady just kept on going. It was terrible. She said she hoped my mom didn't have more children because she didn't want more people like us in the country. My mom started to tear up, and looked away from the lady. So did everyone else. No one on the bus said or did anything.

I also often hear comments about how well-spoken I am, and people will ask me where I come from, and when I say America, they will ask me again: "But where are you *really* from?" They seem surprised that I can be intelligent and well-spoken and still be Black and American.

LINDA: But, isn't it okay to ask people where they came from? I'm really interested in geography, so I love to learn where people's ancestors were born. I'm not trying to be racist when I ask—I'm just curious. And the thing about your English is just a compliment, right? It doesn't have anything to do with skin color or racism, does it?

THANDIE: Being curious is totally fine. But "where do you *really* come from?" makes me feel like I don't belong here. How many times has someone commented on how well you speak English? Or asked where you *really* came from?

LINDA: It's never happened to me. You've lived your whole life here so in a way you're more American than me, and you still get questions that I've never been asked. I'm

embarrassed that it never happens to me and yet it happens to you.

THANDIE: Why do you think that is?

Why do you think that Thandie and Linda have such different experiences of racism? If you are not sure why, talk to your parents, teachers or another adult.

What would you have done if you'd been on the bus with Thandie and her mother that day?

- Would you have told the lady that this isn't how we talk to each other? Would you have said to her that what she was saying was racist and unacceptable?

- Would you have notified the bus driver at the next stop about what was happening?

- Would you have asked Thandie and her mother if they were alright and if there was anything you could do to help them?

- If you had done just one of these things, that's great! You'd get extra points for doing all three. But what matters most is that you acted like an anti-racist and did **SOMETHING**!

"There comes a time when silence is betrayal."

DR. MARTIN LUTHER KING JR.

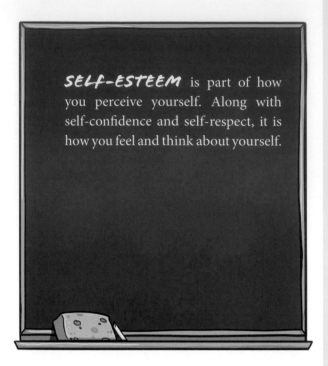

SELF-ESTEEM is part of how you perceive yourself. Along with self-confidence and self-respect, it is how you feel and think about yourself.

TINASHE: After living through racism during my childhood, my self-esteem and self-confidence were very low. I struggled to accept who I was, and often felt worthless. I was reminded, on a daily basis, that there was something different about me and that this difference was somehow wrong. Racism can make you feel like you're being punished for something you can't control, and that no one can do anything about, namely the skin color you were born with. Racism is painful, and in the worst cases, it can be life threatening.

For those who haven't experienced racism, it's not always easy to understand how dangerous it can be. However, all you have to do is read the newspapers or watch television or follow social media to see how widespread racism—and violence around racism—is in the United States.

Recent racially motivated killings in the United States

Emanuel African Methodist Episcopal Church shootings. On June 17, 2015, Dylann Roof shot and killed nine Black Americans at the Emanuel African Methodist Episcopal Church in Charleston, South Carolina. Roof, who is a white supremacist—which is the belief that white people are superior to other races—specifically targeted the historically Black church.

In 2016, Roof was convicted of multiple hate crime and murder charges. He is currently serving a life sentence in prison.

George Floyd was a Black American man who was murdered on May 25, 2020, by several police officers in Minneapolis, Minnesota, while being arrested for allegedly using a counterfeit twenty dollar bill. During the arrest, Derek Chauvin, one of the officers, who was white, knelt on the handcuffed Floyd's neck and back for 9 minutes and 29 seconds, which caused his death. Floyd's dying words were, "I can't breathe." His murder led to mass protests against police brutality throughout the United States, as well as the rest of the world. Chauvin was sentenced to over twenty years in prison for murder and manslaughter.

Buffalo supermarket shooting. On May 14, 2022, an eighteen-year old white man named Payton S. Gendron shot and killed ten people and injured three more at a supermarket in Buffalo, New York. All of the victims were Black. Like Dylann Roof, Gendron was a supporter of white supremacy. On February 15, 2023, Gendron was sentenced to eleven consecutive life sentences in prison without the possibility of parole.

Racism Can Kill

These are just a few of the many examples of how deadly racism can be. As we can see, attitudes like white supremacy often lead to violence. And it is not just Black people who are victims of these attitudes, but also Asian Americans, Latinos, and other non-white groups.

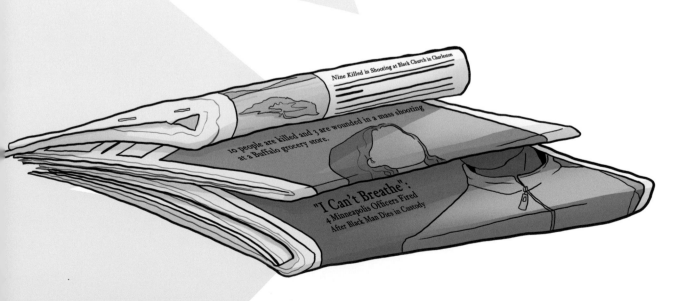

"Every great dream begins with a dreamer. Always remember, you have within you the strength, the patience, and the passion to reach for the stars to change the world."

HARRIET TUBMAN

DID YOU KNOW that discriminating against a person because of their race is illegal in the United States? According to the US Department of Justice, you are not allowed to discriminate against someone because of where they come from, their race, color, religion, disability, sex, culture or language. This means people cannot be denied "equal opportunity" because they or their family are from another country, have a name or speak with an accent associated with a particular group, because they participate in customs associated with a certain group, or because they are married to or spend time with people of a particular group.

Racist views aren't just nasty, they can also be deadly. People's lives are at stake if we allow racist attitudes to flourish.

WE CAN SAVE LIVES BY BEING ACTIVE ANTI-RACISTS!

Skin color—What actually is it?

Human skin color is determined primarily by the amount and type of *melanin* pigment the skin contains; and it varies, from pale pink to almost black. Brown and black-skinned people don't have more pigment cells than white-skinned people, but their pigment cells do contain more melanin.

Did you know that people with melanin-rich skin need six times more sun to get enough vitamin D than white people do? So people with melanin-rich skin, who live in places where there is very little sun, are advised to take vitamin D supplements!

THE MORE MELANIN YOU HAVE IN YOUR SKIN, THE DARKER YOU ARE. YOU CAN REFER NICELY TO PEOPLE WITH A LOT OF MELANIN IN THEIR SKIN BY SAYING THEY HAVE MELANIN-RICH SKIN. SOME PEOPLE PREFER TO REFER TO THEMSELVES AS BROWN OR BLACK.

Skin color is also connected to geography, and can be different according to how sunny it is where you live. For example, there is a lot of sunlight around the equator, so people who come from there will often have darker skin. People from snowy areas (such as the Arctic) also tend to have darker skin because the sun's rays are reflected by the snow. It is a form of protection against the sun's strong ultra violet (UV) rays, just like sunscreen. It is basically the skin protecting itself.

Research shows that the first humans (who we call *homo sapiens*) evolved in Africa. Human fossils (the remains or traces of life), dating back almost 200,000 years, have been discovered in the African countries of Chad, Ethiopia, Kenya and Tanzania. It wasn't until 100,000 years ago that these people began migrating north. During this migration, human skin color changed. When humans reached Northern Europe, they didn't need the same protection from the sun's rays because there isn't as much sun there. Over the course of many generations, their skin color became lighter and lighter, to make it better at absorbing vitamin D from the available sunlight.

THANDIE: I remember the first time I thought my skin color was "wrong." I was in kindergarten, and everyone at my table was drawing a picture of themself. The white children used a crayon named "skin color" to draw themselves. However, the crayon I used to draw myself was the color of what the other kids called poop. Because there was a color called "skin color," which didn't look like my skin, I thought my skin color had to be wrong. It was the first time I remember feeling bad about how I looked.

TINASHE: We have to stop referring to crayons, tights, bandages and other things as *skin color*, because skin colors come in many different shades. When we refer to a particular color as skin color, we are saying that other colors are not acceptable skin colors.

A few years ago, one young girl did something about this!

In 2019, when she was in third grade in Virginia, eight-year old Bellen Woodard noticed that when her classmates asked for the "skin color" crayon, they were asking for the peach-colored one, which was also known as flesh-colored. As the only Black girl in her class, Bellen knew that the peach crayon did not represent the color of *her* skin.

Bellen decided that when one of her classmates asked for the skin color crayon, she would ask them what they color they wanted, instead of just giving them the peach-colored crayon. Soon, her classmates starting asking for the color that they felt best represented the color of their skin!

If the kids in her class could do this, Bellen thought that kids in other schools could, too.

THIS IS WHAT SKIN-COLORED PENCILS LOOK LIKE

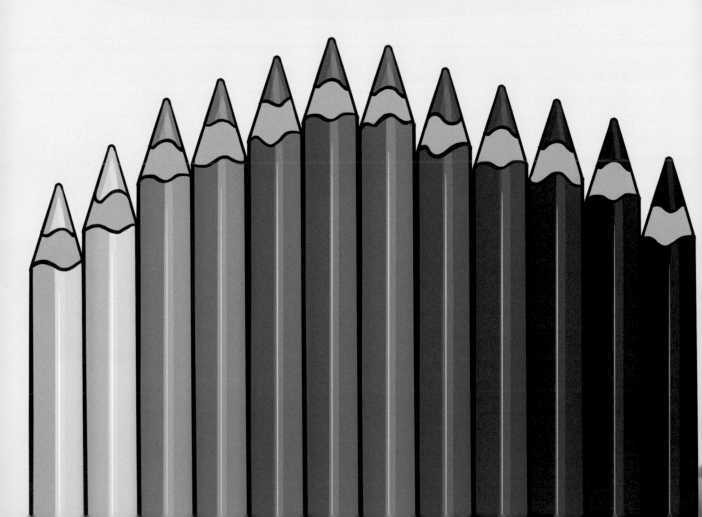

So she came up with "More than Peach," which were drawing kits that could be donated to kids who couldn't afford art supplies. Each kit had a drawing pad, a postcard from Bellen, a regular box of crayons (or colored pencils) and a special box of multicultural crayons (or colored pencils.) While peach was one of the colors in the box, so were other colors, including "apricot," "burnt sienna" and "mahogany."

Eventually, Bellen wrote a book, also called *More Than Peach*. And, because of her anti-racist activities, there is now a crayon box called "Colors of the World." Bellen says that, "[i]nstead of asking kids what they want to be when they grow up, ask them what they want to change."

HOW CAN WE TALK ABOUT BEING DIFFERENT IN A POSITIVE WAY?

!

Remember
skin color says nothing about who you are as a person!

TINASHE: Do you remember when we talked about structural racism, about something only being made for one specific group of people? This applies when we talk about skin color, too.

There are many different skin colors, but it took a long time before products that were supposed to be "skin color" (such as bandages, tights, crayons and makeup) became available in different tones and were not just made for people with white skin. Have you ever considered how a beige-colored bandage, like those you find in most stores, is highly visible on darker skin? The whole point of the color of a bandage is for it to be invisible!

TINASHE: As we have seen, skin color has many different shades, and how dark someone is depends on how much melanin they have in their skin. Traditionally, people with darker skin come from the equator and the Arctic. But today, people with every type of skin color live all over the world, which means you can't tell where someone comes from just by the color of their skin. And if you go back in time, we all came from the same regions, anyway. Imagine, just 100,000 years ago—which in a historical sense isn't very long—everyone had dark skin!

LINDA: My mother always gets really brown during the summer. Does that mean we are originally from someone other than Germany?

TINASHE: Not necessarily. If you spend a lot of time in the sun, the UV-rays eventually start to burn your innermost layer of skin. Your body responds to this by producing melanin, which makes the skin darker. So your skin will become browner than it was before your body started producing melanin.

People often ask if I can get sunburned, and the answer is yes, I can. Darker skin is more resistant to the sun, but we can all get sunburned, so it's important to always use sunscreen!

LINDA: I've noticed that no matter your skin color, everyone has pale skin on their palms and under their feet. Why is that?

TINASHE: It's because there are no pigments in those places. Remember, no matter how brown your skin gets during the summer, you are still pale in the places that are not exposed to the sun.

Exercise

Go to the kitchen and find two glasses, and two eggs, one white and one brown. Break the white egg into one of the glasses and the brown one into the other glass. What's the difference? Nothing, they're both eggs, with the same yellow yolk on the inside!

You now have two eggs, and since it's never good to waste food, you can make yourself an omelette! To do that, you will also need:

> *2 tablespoons of whole milk*
> *1/4 teaspoon of salt*
> *1 tablespoon of butter*
> *2 slices of ham, coarsely chopped (or some vegetables, if you don't eat meat)*
> *1 pound, grated cheese*

What to do:
- Whisk the eggs, milk and salt together.
- Melt the butter in a frying pan until it sizzles. Pour in the egg mixture.
- Fry the omelette by pushing everything into the middle so that any part that's still runny comes into contact with the pan.
- Add the ham/veggies and cheese when the omelette is almost finished.
- Fold it all over and put it on a plate.

Yummy!

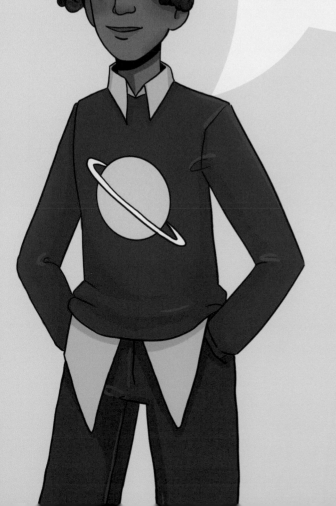

Prejudice

A prejudice is a *preconceived* attitude or idea about a group of people that is not based on real experience. Prejudices are usually negative, and can be due to someone not knowing much about the people or the group.

An example of prejudice is when an airport security guard checks black or brown-skinned people more closely than white people because they believe that people with darker skin are more likely to be criminals.

Prejudices are almost always wrong, and can be very damaging in many ways.

Stereotypes

A stereotype is a belief that all people belonging to a particular group act in a similar way and have the same abilities. These beliefs often concern nationality, ethnicity, gender or skin color. Typical stereotypes are how Asian people are good at math, Black or Brown people are good at dancing and sports and that boys only like playing with cars and that girls only like playing with dolls.

STEREOTYPES VS. PREJUDICES

The difference between *stereotypes* and *prejudices* is that while stereotypes can change over time as people become more familar with a group or culture, prejudices are more difficult to get rid of because they are not based on real life experience.

We can say that all prejudices are stereotypes, but not all stereotypes are prejudices.

VAISHALI: I can understand why being prejudiced is wrong, but I don't see the harm in some of these stereotypes. Why is it bad to say that someone is good at math or dancing. Is there something I'm not getting?

TINASHE: While some stereotypes might seem harmless, or even positive, when you judge a person simply based on their skin color or where they come from, but not on who they are or their actual abilities, that can be very hurtful. What if you are Asian-American, but find math difficult? Or if you're like me, with brown skin, and can't dance? The truth is that we cannot judge a person based only on how they look or where they're from.

Prejudice—to pre-judge

The word prejudice is derived from "pre" (as in, before) and "judge." A prejudice is when you make a decision about someone's abilities or interests without knowing anything about them as a person. If you don't know anything about a person, or have never even talked to them, then you can only judge them based on a stereotype, which is wrong.

Prejudices are not always racist. Imagine, for example, that you see someone on the subway and they're wearing ratty old clothes and smell bad. You might think that that person is poor, and could be homeless. If you thought those things, then you are being prejudiced.

Prejudice can also be about someone's ability to function. Maybe you have seen a person in a wheelchair, and thought about how they can't participate in sports. That is also being prejudiced. You have drawn conclusions about who the person is based on nothing but their appearance.

It is important to point out that prejudices can sometimes be used to protect ourselves. If a girl goes out alone at night and is extra careful when she notices that a man is following her, she is protecting herself. But in most situations, prejudice is discriminatory, hurtful and harmful.

There is an expression about giving someone "the benefit of the doubt." This means that you choose to believe the most positive thing about that person if you don't know any better. So, if you are ever in a situation where you meet someone who looks a particular way, and you assume that that person belongs to a certain group, ask yourself: Can I really know this for sure, just from the way this person looks? If not, try to give them the benefit of the doubt!

Xenophobia means being frightened of people or customs that are from a different country or culture. Many people with xenophobia are afraid of people who look or act differently than they do. Xenophobia often stems from not knowing much about the person or culture. An example of xenophobia can be someone saying, "These foreigners are coming to our country and taking our jobs!"

THEY'RE TAKING OVER OUR COUNTRY

MIGRANT CRISIS

Talk among yourselves

Have you been prejudiced against a person or group?

If so, why did you feel this way, and where do you think that feeling came from?

REPRESENTATION AND DIVERSITY — WHY IS IT SO IMPORTANT?

Diversity means that people from different cultures and ethicities are *represented* in all apects of society, including employment, eduation and entertainment. Diversity isn't just about skin color; it also includes gender, religion, sexual orientation, a person's disabilities and language. Diversity enriches our society in so many ways. Imagine how boring it would be if we were all exactly the same!

TINASHE: As an adult, I've thought a lot about why I spent so much of my childhood wanting long blonde hair, blue eyes and a narrow nose. I hated my big lips and my curly hair. And I thought my nose was too wide. But why did I feel like that? Because when I was growing up, I never saw anyone like me on television or in magazines. The only dolls I had were white, because that was all you could get back then. The characters in my school textbooks had "regular" names like Lisa and Michael.

The images that I saw that were supposed to represent "beauty" didn't look like me at all.

So, the next time you watch a movie, TV show or read a book or magazine, ask youself, how diverse is it?

Cultural diversity in books, magazines, television, movies or other types of media is important because it allows kids with different backgrounds to see themselves represented in the larger world, and also exposes white children to a variety of different skin colors and cultures. This helps them understand that it's as natural to have a Black or Brown person star in a film, or be the main character in a book.

Diversity and representation isn't just important in media, it's also important in your regular life. How much diversity is there among your circle of friends, your parents' friends, on the street where you live and among the kids in your school and your teachers? Diversity is important because it gives everyone a chance to see themselves represented in all aspects of life!

Be aware, make a difference! Next time you are thinking of buying your little brother or sister a gift from the toy store, notice how many dolls with non-white skin colors are on the shelves, or how many diverse books there are. If the store seems to be lacking in these areas, you can actually make a difference. Ask at the checkout counter if they can start stocking a more diverse range of books and dolls. If we all do this as customers, businesses will have to listen to us and we can get everyone represented!

In what ways do YOU think diversity has enriched our society?

LINDA: As a white girl, I have seen families on television that look like mine my whole life. It is so common, I don't even think about it.

JASMINE: My family is originally from Vietnam, and I hardly ever see families from there on the shows I watch. While my parents tell me things are better than when they were growing up, most people I see on TV don't represent me.

LINDA: It must be really hard to watch television and never see yourself represented.

JASMINE: It is. And its not just me. There are so many groups in the world that are not represented on TV and in movies and books!

ZACK: In America, most of our ancestors originally came from somewhere else, so it is important that when we turn on the TV, or watch a program on our phone or iPad, or read a book, that we see everyone represented!

JASMINE: I know that I would feel more included if I saw more families

similar to mine on TV, or in magazines and films. And other types of families, of course!

LINDA: Thanks so much for sharing this with me. I think I now understand how important diversity and representation are; it allows everyone to feel at home—literally!

Here is a Bingo game that you can play with a friend while watching a show.
Can you get four in a row?

diversityBINGO

IS TRANS	USES A WHEELCHAIR	IS OVERWEIGHT	WEARS GLASSES
SPEAKS MORE THAN TWO LANGUAGES	IS A VEGETARIAN	IS MUSLIM	SPEAKS SIGN LANGUAGE
HAS MORE THAN THREE SIBLINGS	IS OLDER THAN 70	IS GAY, LESBIAN OR BISEXUAL	HAS RED HAIR
IS ADOPTED	HAS PARENTS THAT ARE THE SAME SEX	HAS AN INTELLECTUAL DISABILITY	IS BLACK!

SAMMY: One day at school we were told to write down all the non-American dishes we ate in a week. There were so many! It then dawned on me just how important diversity is. Think, without immigration and diversity, there would be no pizza, or sushi or my favorite night at home, taco Tuesday!

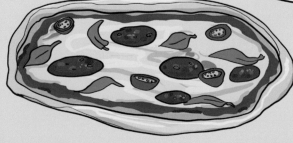

"Be the change you want to see in the world."

MAHATMA GANDHI

When we talk about racism, we often focus on our differences. But it's actually much nicer to talk about our many similarities.

Look at the illustration below and indentify one of the things that the group has in common. Hint: We all love pizza, don't we!

Talk among yourselves

What does representation and diversity mean to you?

ALLIES — STEP FORWARD!

Being *allied* with someone means joining forces with them to achieve a common goal. What's the best way for you to be an ally in the fight against racism?

SAMMY: I usually walk with my friends to and from school. One day, on our way home, we passed a group of high school boys. They stopped us and asked why there was such a strong smell coming from us. We didn't understand what they meant, so we just shrugged and said we didn't know. Then, in a really loud voice, one of the boys said, "It's probably because you're hanging out with him." They boys then looked at me. I knew I had been singled out because I wasn't white, like the other boys. They all started laughing.

I looked down at the ground, while one of my friends looked away, and another stared at his phone. After the older boys finally left, one of my friends asked if we should go get some pizza. None of my friends said anything about what had just happened. I've never felt more alone.

ANTON: I find it hard to say anything during conversations about racism because I don't really feel like I've got anything to share. I would like to help, and at least speak out when I see someone being exposed to racism, but I feel like it would be awkward. It's somehow not "my fight," and even though I'd like to say something, I don't feel like I can.

SAMMY: When the high school boys picked on me, the worst thing was how my friends didn't say anything. I understand them not saying anything directly to those boys, because they were older than us and scary, but they didn't say anything to me afterwards. I know that my friends support me, but I just felt really let down by them. They could have at least asked if I was alright.

ANTON: Like me, I don't think your friends knew what to do, and when that happens, it's easy to do nothing. I've been in that situation myself. If I'd been with you that day, what could I have done?

"In the end, we will remember not the words of our enemies, but the silence of our friends."

MARTIN LUTHER KING JR.

TINASHE: An ally is someone who gives you their support even if the issue doesn't concern them directly. Racism, prejudice and xenophobia aren't just a problem for Black or Brown people. They are everyone's problem, and we can't do anthing about them unless EVERYONE is involved.

HERE ARE SIX SUGGESTIONS ABOUT HOW TO BE A GOOD ALLY

1   Read about racism and its history. Look for books, articles and films on the subject. You don't know where you are going until you know where you've been!

2   Listen to people who have felt the impacts of racism and try to learn from them. Don't respond to their stories with comments like, "They didn't mean any harm" or "Don't be so sensitive." Stories about racism are hard to tell, so consider it a show of trust that they want to share their story with you.

3   Pay close attention to your social circle. What kind of attitudes do your friends and family share? Speak out when you hear racist comments—even when people with a different racial identity than you aren't there.

4   Don't be afraid to be in an uncomfortable situation. It's not always easy to call out someone who is being racist or who has a racist attitude, but it is so important. Don't be afraid of creating a bad atmosphere. Saying no is a key part of being a vocal anti-racist!

5   Learn from your mistakes. No one is perfect, and we all make mistakes from time to time. The most important thing is to learn from your mistakes and not repeat them.

6   Get involved! Whether it's a demonstration, protest, social media campaign, petition or candlelight vigil—all of which we will soon learn about—be clear about what YOU stand for!

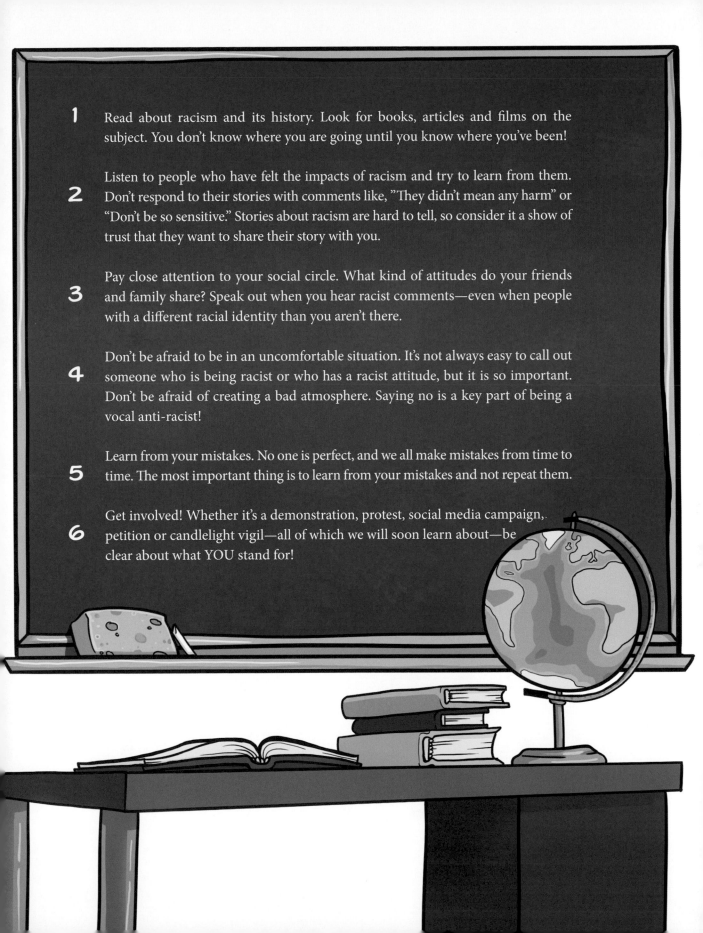

Talk among yourselves

Have you been in a situation where you either needed an ally or were an ally yourself?

When you witness racism, it is important to DO SOMETHING!

DEMONSTRATING AND PROTESTING
— DOES IT REALLY MATTER?

A *demonstration* is when people join together publicly in support of an issue or cause.

A *protest* is when people join together publicly *against* a particular cause or issue.

VAISHALI: A couple of years ago I took part in a demonstration for the environment that had been arranged in connection with Greta Thunberg's school strike. I thought it was important at the time, although it didn't feel like much happened afterwards. I don't think it helped or changed anything. Why is it so important to demonstrate?

TINASHE: It can take a long time from the start of a movement until we see any kind of change. However, demonstrations and protests are important because they bring people together for a common goal, which is the first step toward change.

The largest protests in American history occured in the wake of George Floyd's murder in 2020. It is estimated that over 25 million people joined in demonstrations across the country. The protests spread worldwide, including to the United Kingdom, Spain, France and Italy.

My home country of Norway got involved as well. On June 20, 2020, thousands of demonstrators gathered outside the parliament building in Oslo to protest police violence and racism. The demonstration, like the others throughout the world, sent a message that police brutality against Black people was unacceptable, no matter where you live!

Although the protests in the wake of George Floyd's murder haven't put an end to racism or police brutality, they sent a message to those who feel the effects of racism: You are not alone, the rest of us don't accept racism and we are united with you against it.

Another reason that we demonstrate is that it can make us feel safer! In 2001, when I was a teenager, a fifteen year-old boy named Benjamin Hermansen, who had a Norwegian mother and a Ghanaian father, was killed because of his race. After his murder, I hid my face in the hood of my jacket and kept my hands in my pockets to prevent anyone from seeing the color of my skin. Then, a few days after the killing, a candlelight vigil against racism was held in Oslo. Over 40,000 people took part. The protest showed the frightened girls and boys in our country that it was safe for them to show their faces and that we all stood together against racism. I walked around with my hood down after that. So, while you may wonder if there's any point in demonstrating or protesting, keep in mind that by doing so you are collectively declaring what kind of world you want to live in and what kinds of things you won't tolerate!

There are many types of demonstrations and protests

Political and Social Justice

Political issues you can demonstrate about include climate change, anti-war and workers' rights. Social justice protests include those against racism, police brutality, such as Black Lives Matters, women's rights and LGBTQ+ rights. The success of a demonstration or protest is often measured by how many people attend.

There have been many famous political and social justice protests in American history. Over sixty years ago, on August 28, 1963, over a quarter of a million people attended the March on Washington, which protested discrimmination against Black Americans and other marginalized groups. It was at this event that Martin Luther King. Jr. delivered his "I Have A Dream" speech.

Candlelight Vigil

A *candlelight vigil* or procession is a peaceful event where people gather together, often carrying candles or other lights, in memory of a tragic event. They may also be held to call attention to the suffering of a marginalized person or group.

A recent example of a candlelight vigil in the United States happened in Charlottesville, Virginia, in August, 2017, in memory of Heather Heyer. Heather was killed a few days earlier when a white supremacist drove his car into a crowd during the Charlottesville racist march and counterprotest.

Social media

Social media can be an effective way to get together and communicate a viewpoint or raise an issue. By using the hashtag symbol (#), you can show your concern about an issue without having to show up physically. This allows people all over the world to share their feelings—and we all know that there is strength in numbers!.

On June 2, 2020, to draw attention to racism in light of the Black Lives Matter movement, over 20 million people worldwide posted a black square on Instagram and tagged it with #blackouttuesday. The black square signified peoples' disgust at police violence and racism —and since black squares were almost the only thing visible when you scrolled through Instagram that day, the action had a significant and poweful impact all over the globe!

Petitions

A *petition* is when you collect as many signatures as possible in support of a cause. The signatures are then shown to politicians so they can see how many people support the cause, in order to bring about change. A petition can be done online, or in-person.

A petition is the reason for Black Lives Matter. In 2012, an unarmed seventeen-year-old Black teenager named Trayvon Martin was killed in Florida by George Zimmerman, a neighborhood watch leader. After his murder, Trayvon's parents started an online petition calling for the arrest of Zimmerman. More than 2 million people signed the petition. Civil rights activists, politicians and protesters rallied behind Trayvon's family and took to the streets to protest his killing. Eventually, Zimmerman was arrested and charged with murder, though he was later found not guilty. Black Lives Matter was started in response to the not guilty verdict.

Boycott

A *boycott* is the act of protesting against a country, business or person by not buying their products or trading with them until they change the way they act. A boycott means that you are saying, "I'm not supporting you until you start behaving yourself!"

For many years, there was something called *apartheid* in South Africa. This was a legal system that separated people according to their race, so that white people and Black people couldn't sit on the same benches, attend the same schools or eat at the same restaurants.

In 1975, the United Nations asked for a worldwide boycott of South Africa. After that, many countries refused to buy South African products, and the country was banned from taking part in many activities. The UN did this to pressure South Africa to end apartheid.

Although it took a while, South Africa finally made apartheid illegal in 1994. And, the most famous anti-apartheid protester, Nelson Mandela, eventually became president of the country!

TINASHE: My grandfather lived in South Africa and experienced life under apartheid. He wasn't allowed to use the same bathrooms or shop at the same stores as white people. There were even signs on park benches and at bus stops that said "whites only," which meant he could not use them.

It's crazy to think that apartheid only became illegal thirty years ago!

Exercises

You learn that a store near where you live treats its Black employees worse than its white workers. You want to tell the store that this is not okay. What is the best way for you to do this?

Some of the parents at your school think you are not being taught enough about inclusion and diversity, and they want to show the school administration that there are many others who feel the same way. What is the best way for them to demonstrate?

A girl in Germany has been punched and dragged by her hijab on her way to school. It has sparked a global campaign called "I wear what I want," and you would like to show your support. How can you best do that?

Going against the flow can pay off! Rosa Parks protested against racism just by sitting down!

Rosa Parks

On December 1, 1955, Rosa Parks got on a bus in Montgomery, Alabama, and sat in an empty seat. Then another passenger came along and told Rosa she had to move because the seat she was sitting in was reserved for white people. Rosa refused to move, and was arrested. Imagine that! She was arrested simply because she sat down and refused to move. This was her protest against discrimination and racism. Her silent protest attracted international attention, and motivated other people to get involved. Rosa Parks' protest is considered an important part of what was known as the American civil rights movement. Using your voice—or in this case, sitting down—can make a difference, as Rosa showed the world!

Another example is the football player Colin Kaepernick. On September 1, 2016, Kaepernick started going down on one knee during the national anthem to protest the racism and abuse of power by the police. Some people felt that he was being disrespectful towards his country, but he also received a lot of support. However, he hasn't been allowed to play football in the NFL for many years because of his actions!

TINASHE: In the 1950s and 1960s, *the civil rights movement* strived to give Black people and other minorities in the United States the same rights as white Americans. The movemement fought for many things, including fair elections and an end to racial discrimination. Dr. Martin Luther King Jr. was the most visible leader of the movement. Several important laws against discrimmiation were passed because of the civil rights movement, including the Civil Rights Act of 1964 and the Voting Rights Act of 1965.

Talk among yourselves

Ask your parents what they know about the civil rights movement?

If you have older relatives, like grandparents, ask them what they remember about the civil rights movement.

In addition to Dr. Martin Luther King Jr., some of the famous figures of the civil rights movement include Bayard Rustin, John Lewis, James Farmer, A. Phillip Randolph, Roy Wilkins and Whitney M. Young Jr.

The movement began in 1954 when the US Supreme Court declared in the case, *Brown v. Board of Education,* that segregating public schools by race was unconstitutional.

The Civil Rights Act of 1964 banned discrimmination on the basis of a person's race, skin color, religion or national origin.

Before the Civil Rights era, Black people and other marginalized groups were often prohibiting from voting. *The Voting Rights Act of 1965* made race-based restrictions on voting illegal.

On April 4, 1968, Dr. King was killed in Memphis, Tennessee. A week later, on April 11, 1968, the *Fair Housing Act* was passed, which banned discrimmination in housing.

DID YOU KNOW?
In the United States, you can demonstrate amd protest in public places such as streets or on sidewalks. You don't need a permit from the police as long as you don't block automobile or pedestrian traffic.

Have you ever seen a demonstration or protest, or taken part in one?

INSPIRING PEOPLE

Dr. Martin Luther King Jr.
One of the leaders of the civil rights movement. He gave the famous "I Have A Dream" speech. Dr. King was shot and killed in 1968.

Ruby Bridges
The first Black American child to attend the all-white William Frantz Elementary School in Louisiana. Bridges was confronted by several white protesters who did not want her to go to school with white students. Things became so bad that she had to have police protection at school. All but one teacher refused to teach her, but she still completed school! Today she is an active anti-racist.

Nelson Mandela

South Africa's first Black president, and a major opponent of apartheid. Mandela was imprisoned for twenty-seven years before he was released and elected president. In 1993, he was awarded the Nobel Peace Prize.

Rosa Parks

Black civil rights activist who refused to give up her seat on a bus for a white person, something that was illegal at the time. Her protest was the start of "The Montgomery Bus Boycott."

Kamala Harris

The first female, Black and Asian Vice President of the United States. Her family is from India and Jamaica, and she is a trained lawyer. Before becoming vice president, she was a senator from California.

Amanda Gorman

A young poet who became known for her poem, "The Hill We Climb," written for Joe Biden's presidential inauguration in 2021. Gorman said that the poem "came to life" after she witnessed the riots that took place on January 6, 2021.

Malala Yousafzai

A Pakistani girl who was shot by a Taliban gunman while on her way to school in 2012. The Taliban do not believe that girls should get an education. Malala survived, and in 2014, was awarded the Nobel Peace Prize at the age of seventeen, becoming the youngest ever winner of the prize. Today she campaigns for the educational rights of girls all over the world.

Be quiet, Uncle Bill!

Standing up to racism from someone you don't know can be hard enough, but it is even harder to say something to friends and family when they make racist comments. Especially when it is someone we love and trust, and who is much older than us.

So what should we do if a relative uses the n-word to describe a Black person? Or if mom or dad say: "If they don't like it here, they can go back to where they came from." Can and should we say something to these kinds of remarks?

The answer is of course YES!!

LINDA: Last Christmas, my whole family was sitting around the dining room table, eating dinner. At one point, my mother said that she'd had a conversation with the neighbors about how cold it had been the past few days.

"Which neighbors?" asked my Uncle Bill.

"The ones who live across the street," Mom replied.

"Ah yes, the [n-word]," Uncle Bill said.

Everyone seemed very uncomfortable with what my uncle had said, but nobody said anything to him. During the rest of the dinner, my uncle said the n-word three more times. I didn't know what to do. I was brought up to respect adults, and I thought that my uncle should know better. But I knew that what he was saying was wrong. However, since none of the other adults said anything, I remaind silent.

ANTON: My grandmother is seventy-eight years old, and we visit her almost every Sunday. She is very nice to us and always gives us money or candy. She also has the world's cutest cat, named Scraps because he's always trying to steal your food! But when we visited last Sunday, Grandma told us that she had been to the doctor to get a blood test and that, "The

woman who took my blood was Black, and was wearing some strange thing on her head. I also couldn't undertand a word she was saying. I want to see an American when I'm at the doctor."

Her comments made my stomach hurt. I couldn't believe that my sweet grandmother could talk about people like that. But I didn't say anything. Neither did my mom or dad.

SAMMY: One time, I went on a ski trip with a white friend and her family. My friend's

mother was surprised that I could ski, since I was Black. She then asked me if my father was disappointed that I liked skiing but didn't do other sports like running or basketball, "because people like you are really good at running." I didn't say anything because it was my friend's mother and I didn't want to risk having her hate me, and losing my friend.

LINDA: I've learned a lot from all of you, but when I listen to your stories, it sounds like

there are so many people who still don't understand how racist they can be, even adults. It is very upsetting. It feels like one person, like me, can't make a difference, no matter what I do!

TINASHE: Do you remember how we talked about allies? This is why we need everyone to be an anti-racist. Imagine if you just planted a little seed of doubt in your uncle, your grandmother, your friend's mother, and made them think about what they had said, and about what kind of ideas and attitudes led them to say those racist things. If we all act together, we can make a real difference in the fight against racism!

What would you have done?

Here are some things you can say if you ever find yourself in the same types of uncomfortable situations as Linda, Anton and Sammy.

Linda's Christmas dinner

1: Say out loud to everyone that using the n-word is unacceptable.

2: Take Uncle Bill to the side after dinner and tell him that you're upset about what he said.

3: If you find it difficult to talk to Uncle Bill yourself, ask your mother, father or another adult you trust if they can talk to him for you.

Anton's grandmother

1: Tell your grandmother that we shouldn't talk about other people like that.

2: Ask your mom and dad if they can talk to Grandma.

3: Ask Grandma why she talks about people in that way. Tell her that although you love her, it makes you sad and upset when she talks that way about other people.

No matter what option you choose—or if you say something that is not on the list—remember that there are no wrong answers in these situations. No matter how you handle Uncle Bill, or Grandma or you friend's mother, you are always right—**AS LONG AS YOU SPEAK UP AND SAY SOMETHING!**

As much as it's really difficult to tell those we love that they are doing or saying something wrong, it is also extra important to do so if we are to be true anti-racists! Children need to sometimes help adults open their eyes to the racist views they are sharing.

Sammy's ski trip

1: Tell your friend's mother that when she says those types of things, it makes you feel bad about yourself.

2: Tell your friend's mother that she is stereotyping you, which is wrong.

3: Tell your parents about what happened, so that they can talk to your friend's mother.

"No one is born hating another person because of the color of his skin, or his background, or his religion. People must learn to hate, and if they can learn to hate, they can be taught to love, for love comes more naturally to the human heart than its opposite."

NELSON MANDELA

I AM A PROUD OF WHO I AM!

TINASHE: Sometimes I hear people say that they just see the person on the inside, not the skin color on the outside. Although they may be well-meaning, what they are saying is still wrong. When you see me, I need to you see my skin color, too. Because if you don't see my skin color, you are not seeing the racism I have experienced, and I need you to see it, because that is part of who I am on the inside.

When I was a child, I never felt Norwegian enough, because I wasn't white. To make up for this, I introduced myself as Tina instead of Tinashe because it made me sound more Norwegian. I straightened my hair so that it would hang down smoothly instead of sticking up in an afro. I felt like I had to be a good, well-behaved girl because I wasn't just representing myself, I was representing everyone with a different background.

I am sure that many of you who live in the United States feel the same way. And it isn't fair. You should only have to represent youself!

So I want to tell you—whether you are Norwegian, or American—that just being yourself is enough.

When I was young, my mother tried to teach me that I could be Norwegian and proud of my roots at the same time. But even though she constantly reminded me of this, I still couldn't shake the feeling that I wasn't Norwegian enough. It ate me up, and I was eventually filled with sadness and shame about who I was.

But now I understand that we humans are not just one thing. We are complex, and it is this complexity that makes us who we are. And

Talk among yourselves

Have you been in a situation where someone has said something that upset you? Were you able to speak out? Why/why not?

who you are has nothing to do with your skin color!

I wish I could say that I have always been good at speaking out, standing up for myself and being an active anti-racist. But the truth is, for many years I was afraid. I lacked the language I needed to tell other people what I felt in my heart, especially when I know they might disagree with me, or ignore me.

I hope that this book has given you some of that language, and that you will now be able to go out into the world and use your voice to stand up to racism in its many forms, both obvious and not so obvious.

I look forward to seeing all the wonderful things you will achieve.

And one last thing: Keep your back straight, your head raised, and smile. The world is yours! <3

Thank you!
Dear mom, thank you so much for always trying to teach me to be proud
of my roots – those in Norway and those in Zimbabwe. I figured it out
in the end, and now wear both with pride!

Many thanks to Linda Tinuke Strandmyr at Agenda X (Anti-racist center)
Many thanks to Antonia Lilie (my form teacher at the Rudolf Steiner school in Oslo)

Many thanks to my family, my friends and my husband, Oddi <3.

TINASHE WILLIAMSON is a socially committed author, actress, model and activist. She was voted role model of the year by the Norwegian Vixen Awards, and was nominated as "Name of the year" by Norway's largest newspaper, *VG*. Tinashe's fight for justice and equal rights for all inspired her to write *Handbook for Young Anti-Racists*.

THEA JACOBSEN is a Norwegian-American illustrator, born in Oslo. She studied animation at the University of Greenwich and has worked as a graphic designer, illustrator and character designer. *Handbook for Young Anti-Racists* is her first illustrated book.